The Story of China in Canada

REV. J. C. SPEER, D.D.

© 2012 by Soul Care Publishing All rights reserved. No part of this book is to be reproduced or transmitted in any manner whatsoever, transmitted electronically, or distributed by any means without the written permission of the publisher.

Library and Archives Canada Cataloguing in Publication

Speer, J. C. (James Charles), 1854-1931
    The story of China in Canada / J.C. Speer.

Also issued in electronic format.
ISBN 978-1-927077-08-5

    1. Chinese Canadians--History. 2. Chinese--Canada-- History. I. Title.

FC106.C5S55 2012   971'.004951   C2012-901146-0

Originally published in 1906 by the Department of Missionary Literature, Methodist Church of Canada. This edition published 2012 by Soul Care Publishing, Vancouver, Canada

Some of the statements and ideas presented in this book are included as a historical record only and do not represent the views of the publisher.

Table of Contents

WHEN YOU MEET A CHINAMAN 1

THE CHINESE 6

HOW HE CAME TO US 10

CHINATOWN 17

VICES AND VIRTUES OF THE CHINESE 28

THE CHURCH AND THE CHINESE 36

METHODS OF WORK, PAST AND FUTURE 45

The Story of China In Canada

WHEN YOU MEET A CHINAMAN

In Chinatown

IN almost every part of this Dominion, no matter how near the great centres or how remote from the highways of life and traffic, we come face to face with the sons of the Celestial Empire. Until the passing of the most stringent exclusion legislation, which places a tax of $500 on the head of every Chinese entering our ports, their numbers were increased by the arrival of every ship from the Far East. They have made themselves the neighbors of everybody, and of people of all conditions. Village, town or city seems to be all the same to "John," and he is ready to turn his hand to all kinds of labor, from work in a lumber camp to the draping of a palace parlor.

You cannot escape this ubiquitous foreigner, no matter to what zone you may hide yourself, and we may well predict that no tax wall can be built which will ultimately keep the Chinese out of our land. Not that I would advocate the "open door" to each and all, but an awakened ant-hill., cannot be controlled by the officer of a customs house. You have met him, and you will continue to meet him, in summer and winter; in the city streets and in the remotest settlements of the rural districts; and it may be well that something more than a passing thought be given to this "stranger within our gates."

Of course in his present state of mental darkness the average Chinaman cares not the value of a broken punk stick what you think about him, but for your own sake, and for the sake of this fair land and its attitude to the average Chinaman, who is, after all, possessed of many possibilities which will be developed either upward or downward, it is well to give him a little thought.

When you meet him halt for a moment and consider a few facts about this representative of the Oriental Empire which is to-day exciting the cupidity of most of the foremost nations of the earth. He is the representative of the oldest nation in the world. The histories of Greece and Rome lie well within the limits of a millennium. The history of the Hebrew people may be measured by twice the historic life of the above mentioned nations, and the same is true of a few nations of more modern times. But when one contemplates the history of the nation represented by this Chinaman the others, as to time, dwindle into insignificance. China, as a nation, writes its history in four volumes, each one covering over one thousand years. One naturally asks oneself how many nations have developed, decayed and disappeared since this heathen colossus came to stand upon the earth? "Only a Chinaman," is a common expression from those who have never studied the life story of the Chinese. One is staggered by the stretch of national history which lies to the rear of this people, who are to-day among the most conspicuous, at least in a political sense, of all the peoples of the earth.

REPRESENTATIVES OF A MOST ACTIVE TYPE OF HUMANITY.

There may not be much to admire in the face or figure of this world-wide traveller. But let us not forget that he is a persistent character, and, if there be anything in experience, a large portion of the globe has known him for a decade of centuries longer than almost any other man one meets. The Chinaman can truthfully declare that when Joseph was prime minister in Egypt his nation was a settled Empire with a constitutional form of government, which was, in many respects, far in advance of anything then known on the earth. And we may well respect that people who, through four thousand years have maintained themselves, while nations of the more advanced type have been smothered in the slime of their own moral corruption. Then, throughout that vast stretch of time, while other nations have devoured one another in war, the Chinese, with a few exceptions, have lived in peace .among themselves, and have asked ever that they might be left alone to work out their own national destiny. That there are evils to be laid to the charge of this people no one will deny, but it should be remembered that throughout all the dreary centuries they have gone forward multiplying in numbers, and have not drifted with the many peoples one could name who have lost themselves in the overwhelming forces of the law of "reversion to type."

Then consider that the Chinaman who passes you on the street is a representative of a most active and ingenious type of humanity. The North American Indian, when discovered by the first explorers of this continent, was a savage in the truest sense. Throughout all the ages in which he had occupied this country he had invented little or nothing except those crude and clumsy implements of the chase which were absolutely necessary to provide for his physical needs, and the same may be said of millions of the aborigines of other lands. *[Publisher's Note: The previous statement is included only to illustrate the thinking of the day and in no way represents the views of the publisher or today's society. In 2008 General Conference of The Free Methodist Church in Canada publicly confessed "a role in the oppression of First Nations people.]* But the case of the Chinese is one of surprising genius, for we are informed that it is more than probable the Pharaohs of the days of Moses, and prior to his time, were dressed in silken robes, the material of which was gathered, spun, woven and dyed in China, and sent across the then known world by these inventive and enterprising- people. It is possible that in the days of our Saviour the "seamless robes," which were so costly and so much treasured that the one worn by the Master was a prize for the soldiers at the cross, were from the manufactories of the Far East; and in the palaces of Antioch and Athens, and in the royal functions of

Rome, the Chinese fabric and fine needlework were the material elements which added a gorgeousness to the scene which later writers have tried in vain to describe.

Someone has said that in a trip around the world one of the monuments of antiquity which exhibits marvelous engineering skill is the ancient Wall of China. Built at a time which antedates the birth of our Lord some two hundred and twenty years, it still stands as a monument of skill and perseverance which staggers human belief. Fifteen hundred miles long, and passing through a territory the physical features of which are as varied and difficult as those which our Canadian railways have to encounter in passing from the Atlantic to the Pacific; some twenty feet high, and broad enough at most points to admit of a roadway on the top wide enough for six horsemen to ride abreast, it traverses the prairie and the desert, stretches across deep morasses, and climbs lofty mountain passes. One cannot imagine what it meant, two centuries before the time of Christ, to accomplish such a task, and yet this was the work of the forefathers of the same Chinaman who rocks for gold on the rivers of British Columbia, or who serves as a *chef* in the homes of those who fare sumptuously every day. It has been asserted that these walls contain material sufficient to build a wall of the average height at which it now stands from Halifax to Vancouver. While the inhabitants of Western Europe and the British Islands were but one remove, in point of civilization, from the savage, these people of China were building canals for irrigation and also for transportation. When Columbus discovered America China was enjoying a canal system which put her cities in water communication with most of the important places in the Empire.

Today we are told by those who travel there of the continual surprises which come to them by the evidence of much which tells of an energy and intellectual acute- ness which no other heathen people exhibit. Seventeen hundred walled cities speak unmistakably of forethought and impressive perseverance. We are almost staggered at the statements that "they dug salt wells five thousand feet deep centuries before Solomon was born, and held civil service examinations for office ages before Abraham received the blessing from Melchizedec." But these things are in keeping with what we see of these people in more recent times. Gunpowder and the mariner's compass were the playthings of the Chinese ages before they were thought of in Western Europe.

A GLIMPSE OF CHINA'S GREAT WALL—A MONUMENT OF ANTIQUITY.

Rev J.C. Speer

THE CHINESE

Canal in the Heart of Canton

IT would be manifestedly unfair to compare the Chinese with the peoples who have had the inspiration of the Gospel' of the New Testament, but, on the other hand, it is a mistake to compare the Chinese with the rude barbarians of such lands as Central Africa, where the millions have practically no history worth the writing. One of the most overwhelming facts in connection with the history of this people is the coherency and persistence of the type in its entirety throughout the vast stretches of time since they appeared on the banks of the Yang-tse River.

That there have been revolutions in the government and mighty upheavals along religious lines are undoubted facts, but these have in no way disturbed the onward flow of this ancient ever-widening river of humanity. The Chinaman is the same yesterday and to-day, and we may well believe he will be the same to the end of time unless we give to him the Gospel of the blessed God. Is it any wonder then that the Chinaman looks upon the whole world as his inferior, when he not only considers his country as the most ancient but also that his is the largest homogeneous nation that has been. That there are wide divergences throughout the Empire is true, for the Cantonese cannot converse freely with those who use Mandarin; but with all these minor differences the literature and the constitution of these 400,000,000 units bind them together so that they are Chinese whether you meet them toiling among the rice paddies or wading through the billows of blossom in the flaming poppy farms; whether you meet them in the lowest opium dens of Shanghai or at the high official functions in the sacred precincts of the inner temple at Peking. They are of the one type, and they remain thus when they cross to the lands beyond the sea. There is but one event which changes the Chinaman, and that is the acceptance of the salvation which is through the atonement of our Lord - But of that more later.

A RICE FIELD AND PEASANTS, NEAR CANTON, CHINA.

Another thing which convinces these Mongolian brothers that theirs is indeed the Celestial Empire is the fact that to them its bounds, are unlimited; and while this is a thought at which other mortals can afford to smile, it may be well to remember that China is a little larger than "Mrs. Wiggs' Cabbage Patch." The country stretches through sixty degrees of longitude by forty of latitude. This means that it covers a little less than five million square miles. It is seven times the area of France. It is forty-four times greater than Great Britain and Ireland. One can take a map of China and cut it into one hundred and four pieces, each piece being as large as the map of England; or into one hundred and seventy-six pieces, each as large as Scotland. China is one-third of Asia and one-tenth of the habitable globe. Someone has calculated that if China were cut into a strip of land a mile wide it would make a road so long that it would take a man walking thirty miles each day, four hundred and fifty years to reach the end. Is it any wonder, then, that never having seen nor read of other lands, these people should believe that they are indeed the greatest of all nations on the face of the globe. But it is well to remember that there are others, who are well qualified to speak on this question who do not hesitate to endorse the thought of the Chinese. Mr. J. W. Foster, who is quoted as one of the great diplomatic authorities of America, has said: "It is scarcely an exaggeration, in view of its history and attainments, to assert that no nation or race of ancient or modern times has stronger claims than the Chinese to be called a great people."

It is but recently that the outer world has awakened to the fact that China is a land of untold riches. It is now seen that while the country, for uncounted ages, has supported hundreds of millions of people, there remains untouched vast stores of wealth which must in the future yield to the magic wand of the miner and manufacturer. It is just now coming to light that there are stored in the mountains and deep valleys of the country mineral deposits unsurpassed for bulk and quality in any other part of the earth. These have scarcely been touched by the people of that land, but the time is not far distant when they will realize their own wealth in raw material such as they never dreamed of before. The same may be said of the timber of their forests and also of the fertility of their soil. What a hive of industry this land has always been, although it has been necessarily a toil of a most primitive character; but when the western world has given to these people the modern implements of industry they will be capable of taking their place with the other nations of the world in all lines of commerce. They have the population, they have the territory, they have the raw material, they have the ingenuity and perseverance, and they are the world's most faithful toilers. They but need, added to these possessions, intellectual culture and the Gospel to place them beside the world's greatest modern nations.

The Chinese are a people who have for thousands of years laid great stress upon education. The public offices are always filled by those who have passed the most severe tests in their classics, and while it is true that this means little to those who are advanced in European culture, it nevertheless goes to show that the leaders of thought are anything but indifferent to education, a spirit which means much in the work of bringing a people from darkness to the light of Christian civilization. We do not forget that vast numbers of these are deplorably ignorant, and almost dehumanised, but the nation must be considered as a whole in any enterprise which contemplates its resurrection to a newness of life even nationally understood.

This is but a brief and fragmentary glimpse of the people who have come to abide with us in this new world, and the more microscopically we examine the Mongolian who has come to our shores the more deeply convinced are we that we cannot afford to treat him as a human atom unworthy of serious consideration. Indeed, it is believed by those who have given the best thought to the problem of the Chinese that they will provide the most important questions of national civilization throughout the entire century upon which we have entered.

Rev J.C. Speer

HOW HE CAME TO US

Harbor, Canton, China

IT was a most momentous event that decided the Chinese people to leave their own for other lands. Throughout all the ages they were a "stay-at-home" people, and perhaps in this innate conservatism is to be found one of the strongest elements in this unique race.

But the last century was a time when every nation was tempted to take a peep beyond its own horizon, and China could not escape the mighty impulse to travel.

Two events in this western world were largely responsible for the influx of the yellow toilers from the Orient. The first was the discovery of gold in large quantities on the western shores of this continent. The Chinaman is one who knows values, and the "main chance" is never treated lightly by him. When the disease known throughout the world as la grippe struck the race it is said to have taken only six weeks to pass round the globe, but that speed was no swifter than that with which the news of the finding of gold in the gulches of the Rocky Mountains reached the ends of the earth, and so great was the find reported that whole ranges were said to be filled with the precious metal. This was back in the forties, and for a decade later there was little thought of or talked about on the Pacific slopes but the one matter of gold mining.

It was in 1848 that the first Chinaman came to the Pacific Coast, and by the time the "gold fever" of '50 had taken hold of the people a sufficient number had come to all the cities of the Coast to waft the news to a very large number of their countrymen in China, with whom they were in continual communication. British and American vessels were in regular connection with the coast cities of China, and the Chinese were secured from time to time as helpers on board, with the" result that they were found to be most faithful servants, and capable of great endurance. This naturally led to their being brought to serve on shipboard when on the voyage, and thus landed on this side of the ocean, to become, for the time being at least, toilers side by side with the people from this and other lands for the yellow treasure which our mountains and rivers produced in such vast abundance. Those who came were, for the most part, from the province of Canton, and while there were among them those of the merchant and cultured classes, the bulk of the people were from the lower or laboring' ranks. Every ship arriving from Hong Kong brought not only its burden of tea and Chinese curios and rice, but its full quota of the men who were in a few years to be looked upon as a peril to the Anglo-Saxon race of this land. For a considerable number of years the danger of the Chinaman as an element in the labor market did not come to the front, and John settled himself in blissful ignorance that anybody was ever likely to find him in the way.

One of the things which impresses the most casual observer is the important fact that the Chinaman is no idler. It has been a very general idea that people who are non-Christian in the sense of being heathen are not fond of the proposition of earning their bread by the sweat of their brow, but this is certainly not true of the Chinese. The miners, from every land and of all conditions, soon discovered that here was a man who could not be surpassed in unremitting toil. It goes without saying that he was at a serious disadvantage in the race for gold. He knew nothing of the language, and the people with whom he found himself knew as little of his tongue. The ways of this western world were all the very opposite of his, where the plane and saw are drawn to the workman instead of pushed from him as in this land; and in fact every other work is what one might call left- handed. But he was a worker and careful in what he did, and he often followed after the stampeders of our own country, and in a little while had his bag of dust at the bank, gathered from what others had overlooked.

The second event which attracted the Chinese to our shores was the building of the great transcontinental railway line. It may well be questioned if the Canadian Pacific Railway could have been built within the time limit had it not been for these thousands of Chinese who could perform the necessary labor under conditions which might well deter the European navvy. We think few will deny the untold benefits which have accrued to this Dominion because of the building of this road, and it may be well to remember that while the brains and money were ours, to a very great extent the muscle was Chinese. One of the benefits of his coming to us was that we found out what kind of a being he was, and that in a way and from a standpoint which was impossible under any other circumstances. It must be admitted that the first impressions were not of the most reassuring character. It is a pity that China could not have been represented at the introduction by some of her higher types, but those who believe in a divine providence in such matters think that the overruling of it will be for good. Perhaps the perspective was too short, but we think John has improved under the close range scrutiny. But be he good or bad, in the main these are the events which brought him to this land. No one will say that they were not events which appealed to .a very sane and human element in the nature of this Oriental.

While on this question it may be as well to remind our readers that it would be an error to suppose that mining and railroad- building are the only occupations to which the Chinaman gives himself. Indeed, there are few people who are as capable as the Chinese of being " Jack- of-all-Trades " without the addition of the latter part of the phrase. In the logging camp and in the muddy ditch, in the cord-wood fallow, in the stone quarry and among the coal miners, he takes his place without hesitation. He is one of the best market gardeners to be found anywhere. In the East we know him principally as a laundryman, but he is equally expert as a cook and housekeeper in some of the best and most fastidious homes of the wealthy. In this land he has entered, thus far, but few of the crafts where long years are necessary to the doing of expert work, but he is as capable of this as the best of us. .The works he can produce are such as to cause no little wonder. In the cities of the West, where the real Chinatown is to be found, he is among his own people, and for some others as well, tailor, shoemaker, butcher and grocer. But to no great extent has he gone into manufacturing, and it is not at all likely that in this respect there will be much danger to business for long- years to come; for those who have come to us are of a class who are foredoomed to the lower ranks of life's labor. This is rather a benefit to us than otherwise, for the undeveloped resources of this Dominion are so great and exhaustless that the rough hard toil of bringing forth the raw material, to the hand of the manufacturer will form the largest part of our operations for generations to come.

HE CAN MAKE WONDERFUL SHOES.

This must not be taken as a plea for the open door for the cheap laborer, but it must be taken to imply that if we are to receive these Orientals the laboring class will be of greater use and more benefit than those of the merchant or official classes. There has been a fear abroad that these people would come to our shores in millions, and that this would become a second China. There are not wanting evidences that of late this feeling has been fanned for a purpose far removed from the protection of the Dominion. "The Yellow Peril " is a phrase which has done duty for enterprises many and varied, but we are not the virile people our fathers were if we fear to receive a few thousand of a race considered so far inferior to ourselves. It should always be considered that the Anglo-Saxon blood invariably rises to the surface of the river of life, and that the civilizing power of a Christian people has always been greater than the degrading force of the heathen. And this is particularly the case when the heathen people are transplanted to the soil and circumstances of Christendom. It is a good thing to remember that there are no people in the world who are so instinctively mimetic as the Chinese. They are the most accurate imitators of the families of the globe. In this fact lies their hope if they come in contact with the more advanced races. It is true that they are the most conservative of nations while at home, but it is seen that much of it disappears when they are enlightened and shown the advantage of a change.

It may not appear to the casual observer that the Chinese living in a foreign country have made marked advancement in the customs of their adopted home, but this is largely due to the fact that they, more than any other people, are treated as intruders and barbarians. Such harsh treatment will not tend to wean them of their own, nor wed them to our country and customs. In this country, and in fact in every western Anglo- Saxon country, the Chinese are as much separated from the-people among whom they live as if they were still in their native land. The only, contact is in the matter of business, or in the relationship of master and servant. For the present this is no doubt as it should be, for notwithstanding all that may be said in his favor the average Chinaman who comes to this country is not companionable for the people he serves. He is generally ignorant of our ways, and therefore cannot become a congenial companion to the more intelligent. But the class to whom we refer will never become obtrusive, for throughout long ages they have learned the lesson of place and position too well to forget it in a foreign land. But the educated and Christian Chinaman is in every sense a gentleman, and judged by the measure of his opportunities he is the equal of any foreigner one can meet. The question, then, to the thoughtful man of worldly wisdom, is answered with reference to this human factor in the building up of this new world. As the Chinese are with us and can be made a force in this land for its development, it will be the wisest economy to help them toward this end, and in rendering this aid we are but helping ourselves. He is a human being with muscle and brain. He is willing to render faithful and efficient service. Out of our mountains and valleys he will dig the crude minerals, which he will help to transport to the manufacturers for their refining. Out of the soil of our lands he will assist to bring forth harvests which will fill our granaries and load our trains and steamships for the market, where millions of hungry ones will be fed, and the national treasury be filled. Our limitless forests and exhaustless fisheries need such toil as he is able and willing to give toward their development; and if he should reach in time to higher positions, where he would be employed in the skilled work of the artisan, he must show himself the equal of the Anglo-Saxon or he will not retain such position.

The cry of this Dominion is for a larger population, and it is evident to all who have looked into the matter that the class of people we most need are not those in the professions, but those who are ready to undertake menial and laborious toil. If it should be thought best let us shut the doors against these people, so that no more may enter, but for those who have already come to us, and for those who are born among us of Asiatic parents, let there be shown the spirit of British fair play, and above all the Christian charity and mercy which brought our Master to this cold world. These men are human, and they have been redeemed by that blood in the merits of which alone we expect to find favor. It must not go before us to the "great white throne" that we either ill-used or neglected these men, over whose nation God, in providential care, has reigned throughout four thousand years. It may be the wisest thing, we say, to prohibit their coming to this country, but once here they become, at least for the time being, citizens of our nation, and as such, while compelled to obey our laws, they must be accorded the same protection as ourselves; and if they are most ignorant they are, on that account, the most needy. The quickest and most certain method of placing them where they will cease to be a menace to the wage-earner is to lift them in the shortest possible time to a plane of civilization where their ideals and needs will be of the highest and widest character.

There cannot be a higher nor more intelligent patriotism in this land than that which stoops to lift up and mould into a perfection of Christian character the most lowly and uncultured who may come to dwell among us. One of the undying glories of the Empire to which we belong is seen in the fact that under our flag all men are free and equal; and all are to be encouraged to live in the fullest enjoyment of our glorious liberty.

China fears the foreigner, and not without good reason, but the foreign nations care little or nothing for the wishes of that or any other foreign land, for at the muzzle of smoking tube and point of glittering bayonet we have compelled our admission and the admission of our commerce, even of rum and opium. Is it then a small thing that we receive graciously those who are with us,-and do for them the best that the Gospel spirit dictates? As citizens and Christian people we are face to face with the needs of these fifteen thousand Mongolians, and it is a problem which must be solved by us in the spirit of true Canadians and Christians. It is not our place to say that the government of the country has done nothing but yield to the solicitations of certain influential persons or classes, and enact laws which have made these strangers feel that Christian charity, wherever else it is to be found, is not in the laws which touch the Chinaman.

It is perhaps well that but few in this land understand just what John Chinaman is talking about after he leaves the customs house officer, where he has been compelled to pay the sum of $500 for permission to live on our soil. But it is not our intention to go into the vexed question of the Chinese tax further than to point out that as a Christian nation we should at least remember that this poor man is our brother, and that the same Lord over all is rich in mercy to all who call upon Him, and if we come short of the teaching of our great Master we have no part with him in the establishment of his kingdom on the earth.

The Story of China In Canada

CHINATOWN

Young China Wide Awake

SOMEONE has said that it is not necessary to go out of our own country to visit China, for one can take a trip through Chinatown, as found in any of the Coast cities of this Dominion, and pass in the distance of a couple of blocks into conditions which are practically identical with what one would find in any of the larger or smaller cities in China proper. It is a remarkable fact that some of these quarters are situated in the very heart of the English-speaking cities, a condition which is due to the fact that the Chinese came in at a time when the early residents were about to look for new quarters, their first buildings having become either too cramped or too dilapidated for the growing and up-to-date demands of modern times. The average Chinaman comes to this country with no intention of remaining longer than the time when he can save a little cash, and therefore, as it is with many others when settling but for a brief period of time, the Chinese are in 110 way particular as to the locality or the character of the dwelling. The result is that while Chinatown is generally in the heart of the city it is the most unattractive, squalid and forlorn of all places one can find.

The people who have a laudable ambition to advance and beautify their city have their patience greatly tried by this eyesore, which is often surrounded by the modern buildings of business centres. On the other hand the landlords who can rent these ramshackle places are much more difficult to move than the Chinese merchants. This condition of affairs places the Chinese who come to us at a view-point which is most unfavorable. Those who have visited China will bear testimony that art in architecture is one of the things in which China can have not a little pride, and one may well believe that but for the fact that they are here but for a brief period of time there would be a much better showing. If the people of Chinatown are not pressed by the city authorities they will take little or no interest in keeping their streets in order, so that often in dry weather the "dust is blinding, and in wet the mud is thick and deep. But while on this point it may as well be said that the Chinese, as a class, are not a whit worse than many other foreigners, and we are not aware that they have suffered from diseases which are incident to insanitary conditions more than any other class of people who have come to us from European countries.

One of the things which is striking to the visitor is the absence of women and children. A few there are it is true, but for the most part they are transients, and such as these do not bring their families to our shores. This is a most serious matter, and one of the sound objections which may be raised to the coming in large numbers of these people. It is always a disaster for men to congregate together, whether for a longer or shorter period, without the blessed influences of a home in which there are women and children. This is true of thousands who spend their years in the lumber-camps, and in the mines of the far North and West. It is a poor home indeed that is totally void of some uplifting influence, and as for the most part these Chinamen leave their wives and children in China they are in a most dangerous and degrading environment.

There are a few who have brought their families to this country—men who after they were here for a time either felt that they could not get rich in a day, or who found that this land was a better place to live in than the one from which they came. The laws, until of late, were not such as to deter a man who had lived under Chinese rule, and the earning power of two pair of hands were much greater in Canada than amidst the swarming millions of the home-land. Those who have thus settled down to life with us have shown themselves to be good citizens, or at least as good as they know how to be.

Passing through the streets one sees the children (for there are some) at play with all the enjoyment of our own little ones. The little child has not the dull stolid countenance of the father, but with bright, black, sparkling eyes they scurry out of the way of the white visitor, showing thus early that they have learned the bitter lesson that they are strangers in a strange land. It is pleasing to hear words of our own tongue from these little strangers, and one is reminded that some of them are as much Canadians as are we of Anglo-Saxon speech. Here and there one meets the tottering form of a woman, picking her way to the house of a neighbor. She is the victim of a custom which has been an unmitigated curse to millions of little children and women in the Celestial Empire—that of foot-binding. These women are dressed most artistically, according to the ideals of the fashion-plates of the Chinese. Tiny shoes, most beautifully embroidered, with the sole tapering almost to a point, so -that the foot rolls as on a rocker as the wearer walks on the solid sidewalk. The lower limbs are encased in silk leggings, with a short skirt, and a silk quilted smock over all.

MRS. CHONG AND FAMILY, VICTORIA, B.C.

The Chinese ladies wear no head covering, but seem to find their chief pleasure in the most elaborate toilet. Their blue-black hair is done up so that it will remain for many days. It is decorated with beads and combs, but no hat is ever worn under ordinary circumstances. The weather may be bright or stormy, cold or hot, but none of these conditions could induce the Chinese woman to patronize the milliner. The parasol or umbrella takes the place' of the American hat, and the crowning ornament of women is in this way shown to the best advantage.

Passing the windows one sees the cobbler at work on the paper-soled shoes, using the most primitive implements for his work. Next door will be the butcher of the town, who sells to all and sundry from the animal which has been roasted whole in his great oven. This saves the necessity of every cook in the town cooking a small piece for each meal. Then one comes to the bric-a-brac dealer, and is bewildered by the accumulation of thread, needles, matches, punk-sticks, red paper, bird-kites, tumbling toys and fire-crackers; but time and space would fail me .to write down all that John the merchant has in his little corner store for the curio hunter or for his fellow countryman.

The vegetable store may be next, and one is puzzled at the variety of strange foreign vegetables for sale. Some of them are imported, and some are grown in our own soil. Long roots like those of the golden or white pond lily, turnip-like roots, peculiarly formed cabbages, and a preparation of what .is known as bean-curd, which may or may not be toothsome and nutritious to a Canadian system. Nearby is the dealer in fine silks, and here comes the temptation of the visitor, for the texture, colors and designs are such as to attract a connoisseur in such lines. The artistic quality of the Mongolian mind needs no argument when one has witnessed the needle work and art designs which are the product of China. One thinks of the long months and even years it has taken to accomplish the task of such embroidery.

As we wander through Chinatown we come across the theatre, where the Chinaman finds much of his amusement. We have been told that no woman is allowed to take part in the drama, but where the *role* demands female characters men are provided to fill the place and play the part. This is the outcome of that pseudo sacred- ness with which the Orientals assume to regard the persons of their women. The plays which are most popular are those which have to do with the history of the nation and the events which have given rise to important epochs. To the ordinary listener it is one tumult of conflicting sounds, and even to those who understand the language it is generally one vast incoherency.

Passing an un-curtained window one sees a dozen men around a great dish of boiled rice, and with a dexterity which is positively bewildering these clumsy men are feeding themselves with chop-sticks. It is as near to the proverbial "supping gruel with a knitting needle" as it is possible to get. It is not true, as most of our vegetarian friends assert, that rice is the only food these people eat, for anyone who has had to do with the Chinese knows well that they consume large quantities of fish, fowl and pork. The latter is their staple meat diet, but no people we have ever met are more willing to pay outside prices for fowl for table and sacrificial use than are they. They are by no means vegetarians, as so many people believe, but they can live on rice exclusively when it is necessary so to do. Speaking of the food of these people we remember that they are the world's greatest tea drinkers. On the counters of the stores, over a little charcoal burner, the teapot is kept ready for the cup of tea either to personal friend or customer. Perhaps this is the explanation of the fact that while these people live in the most insanitary squalor, they escape many of the diseases with which those more scrupulous are smitten. They seldom drink raw water, and it is believed that this prevents the taking of those diseases which are communicated by the use of impure water.

One of the most interesting places to be visited in Chinatown is that of the confectioner. The making of confections is a fine art with the Chinese, for they are, above all others, lovers of the sweet and toothsome. The great days, such as Chinese New Year, are times when the people expend large sums on sweetmeats and sugar productions, with many kinds, of dried fruit and nuts. Many of these are not as palatable to the Canadian as to the Chinese; but there is no way to account for human tastes, and we may be well satisfied if they are happy. What numbers of things one misses from these places without which we think we could .scarcely live. The baker and milkman never call at the home of the Chinese housekeeper. The house furnishings are of the most meagre kind, and this seems to be the case among the better-to-do people as well as among the poorer classes.

Perhaps among, all the memories which follow the visitor none will cling so long as that of the odors, which are so numerous that one becomes bewildered as to whether they are good, bad, or indifferent. Someone has described a Chinese smell as "a mixture and a puzzle, a marvel and a wonder, a mystery and a disgust, but nevertheless a palpable fact."

The cause for all this it appears is found in the fact that the opium smoker is not far away, and the other smells, better and worse, filtering through this most abominable stench, produce effects not to be - obtained otherwise. Another memory which one will carry from Chinatown is "that of the sounds, which are ever to be heard day or night, from the outlandish fiddles and the booming of the worshippers' drum, together with the dulcet tones of the tongueless bells. The screech of a Chinese fiddle, or a number of them, is not just like any sound known to the ears of men, and the booming of the drum smites upon the ear with that dull monotony that breeds an unspeakable dread. But over against these we must place the sounds of the bells which are touched by the soft hammer in the hands of the Confucian worshipper. Soft and liquid are these notes, like spirits lost among the discord of the drums and fiddles, and the memories of these tones heal the wounds of the harsh rasping of the other instruments. Heathenism as found in China, and transplanted to our own land, has neither sweet odors nor sweet music, with the one exception of the tongueless bells.

The dead walls are the place for the announcements of the various society meetings, and the notices are in the form of a red strip of paper upon which stand out the curious Chinese characters. Several societies have their headquarters in every Chinatown. Before these billboards there is to be found a crowd of people reading not only the notices of meetings of secret societies, but also many other items of interest which the writers keep posted for the information of the people. They have few if any books and no newspapers, and they read and discuss the notices by the hour.

It is evident that the social instincts of the Chinese are highly developed, for one cannot walk the streets of their towns without encountering groups of men everywhere engaged in conversation, and often in the excitement of good fellowship. One of the most pleasing sights to be witnessed is the attitude of the fathers to their sons, where the family has been established in this country. The affection of a husband for his wife is a quantity which is mostly wanting, but his whole affection seems to be placed on his little sons, and this may in some way account for the obedient reverence of the sons for the father, so that as long as he lives .he remains true, and after the parent is dead the son becomes a worshipper at his shrine.

The Chinaman seems to think his love should be lavished upon his son that he may offer the proper devotion and sacrifices after he himself has departed this life. This is one of the few bright spots in the heathenized nature of the Chinaman. It is true that there are exceptions to this rule, but few husbands among the Chinese seem to think of the wife as higher than a chattel which it is convenient to have. The story is well authenticated by a medical missionary, who called to see a woman who was very sick in a miserable shed, with the rain dripping down upon the fever stricken creature. The doctor appealed to the husband to provide a better place for the sufferer or there would be little hope of her recovery; but the husband. declared that the only dry place was the other shed in which he sheltered his ox, and if it were to be turned out and get wet and die, he would have to buy another, but if his wife were to die it would cost him nothing for another. The missionary declared that there were many million women in China who were married to men who were not a whit better than this one. But, as we have said, the love of little children still burns in the breasts of the fathers, and this is a flame which the Christian religion feeds till it spreads to the whole nature of the darkened heathen.

One cannot leave Chinatown without seeing the Joss House. Victoria, B.C., has two or three, and they stand for heathen worship transplanted to this Christian land. It is worthwhile for those who affect to care nothing for the Christian Church to spend a while in one of these dreary places, that they may feel how far above and beyond this kind of worship is the baldest kind of congregational service in a Christian church. An outer court, which has at its entrance a few smoking, ill-smelling punk-sticks; an aged caretaker who, with the utmost politeness, admits the visitors, many of whom are not over-considerate of the feelings of the "heathen Chinee"; into a large square room, which is shrouded in semi-darkness and filled with the vile odor of the incense which is ever burning or smouldering on the altar, you are conducted. The place is decorated with the colors of the dynasty now on the throne, and the peacock feathers are in evidence. They are well schooled in honoring the reigning monarch. Long strips of red and yellow paper hang from the walls, on which are written prayers or words which indicate that they are for the payment of the demons as a peace offering. On the side of the room, directly opposite the entrance, is a flue or open fireplace, and by the side of it a drum. The worshipper lights his prayer paper, and as it burns the draught of the flue carries it out of sight to the demons which await the offering. To attract their attention the drum is beaten, and its mournful notes awaken strange feelings in those who hear it for the first time in the gloomy precincts of this idolatrous temple. Turning away from the flue one faces the prayer mat upon which the devout Confucian falls, and to which he bows his forehead with many genuflections. In his hands he holds two half-round pieces of wood, in the form of split beans. If he is offering prayers for prosperity in the next cargo of rice or tea, he will, after offering his sacrifice in the form of a swine or a fowl, let fall these prayer sticks, and on the particular way they rest on the mat depends the answer to his supplication. If the answer be unpropitious he may repeat again and again till the sticks fall in the fortunate form, then he is satisfied.

    A moment's observation touches one with the pathos of the whole performance, for the sincerity of the heathen none can doubt, but the childishness of the matter is saddening to those who have learned the better way. On an elaborately carved and gilded altar is the offering to the god or Joss. As intimated, it may be a swine roasted whole, or fowl; it may be tea or some other decoction as drink; but we have never seen the altar without a sacrifice on it in the many times we have been in these places. In a dark recess immediately behind the altar is the god, in the form of a most repulsive Chinese figure, with long black beard. Nothing can exceed the malignant expression of this idol as his dark features are illumined by the light-which flickers from a crystal cup suspended in front by an invisible cord. The shrine is decorated, as are the other parts of the place, with much paper and feathers, which are covered with dust and cobwebs; and the odor of burning punk-sticks, and smell of the half- roasted meat, make the visitor feel that a charnel house is not far away. Depression of feeling to those who visit such places is an almost universal experience, and one there for the first time realizes the delights of worshipping in the Christian forms, where congregations gather as friends, and where to the power and sympathy of numbers are added the inspiring themes of sacred praise and sermonic instruction. The Joss House sees no congregation, hears no song of praise, and no inspiring discourse which lifts the thought and heart to better things for time and eternity, but gloom and uncertainty attend the solitary worshipper through all. Who that has "tasted of the good gift of God, and the powers of the world to come," can withhold pity for a brother redeemed who thus bows down to demons?

The funeral customs of the Chinese are peculiar. One of the most prized gifts that a child can bestow on a parent is a coffin. These may be received at any time in life, and many have stored the coffin in the home for years. On the other hand death has a terror for the Chinese mind of which we know nothing. The upper air being full of demons, who await the death hour, it is believed that the dying one should not be kept in - the dwelling, but in some outhouse. This is a precaution against an invasion of these malignant spirits.

A CHRISTIAN CHINESE FAMILY.
The children are Christians of the third generation.

On this account, instead of the patients passing away among the friends in the home, they are taken to some place where they may escape the notice of these denizens of the upper air. When a person of note and wealth is to be buried; the day is one of the greatest excitement, and large amounts of money have been spent in this country at such a time. In one case which took place in the city of Victoria the street was laid with several platforms, on which were abundance of many kinds of confectionery and other foods.

The secret orders to which the deceased belonged were out in full regalia, with banners and drums, and for hours the funeral services went on in the open street. The priests were dressed in robes of white, and went through numerous ceremonies and offerings of prayers. The funeral cortege was followed for a distance by hired mourners, men dressed to resemble women. Their pig-tails were combed out, and the long black hair, dishevelled and falling to the ground as they bowed down in their assumed grief, made up a scene which was pathetic in the extreme.

After the coffin came the attendant whose duty it was to scatter the "cash-paper," which was to deceive the demons who were after the soul of the departed. The red strips of paper, which were scattered all the way from the house to the grave, were a sort of bogus money which for the time being kept the demons back. When the grave was covered the sacrificed swine was placed upon it as an offering and safeguard. We have been told that in the early days in British Columbia the offering at the grave was left there, but finding that the Indians, without compunction, made a feast of the sacrifice, the Chinese concluded that it was as well for them to bring it home for the same purpose, and this rule is now followed. In all this we behold the tremendous struggle of these dark-minded heathen to get free from the terrors of evil in the world, and ever without finding the way.

Rev J.C. Speer

VICES AND VIRTUES OF THE CHINESE

Young China
A Home Ruler

NO matter how far men travel from their native soil, they carry with them their vices as well as their virtues. The sinful heart of all men everywhere is the same fountain of evil, but the foul streams run in channels which have been made by the customs and environment of national life. This being the case, when the Chinese come to our shores they naturally follow the ways of evil which were common in their own land, unless there are forces at work here which will deter them. The Chinaman in China is an inveterate gambler, and the same man in Canada follows the habit of all his life without any thought that he is doing wrong. We have heard often the loud cry against these people for their fearful tendency to gamble, but it might occur to us that the Chinese have never really been awakened to the wickedness of this practice. From childhood they have practised this ruinous habit in its simpler and more complex forms, and having never been shown that it is wrong to take another's money without giving real value for it they are as dark this as upon a thousand other matters of right and wrong in this new world.

Then when the Chinaman comes here he finds that Christians (?) gamble, and that in very many ways. He sees that so-called Christians (for all who are not heathen are Christian to him) are as fond of dice, cards, horse-ring and wheel of fortune as he, and he is bewildered when the missionary expostulates with him on the ground of moral wrong; and the climax is reached when the policemen raid his house, drag a dozen or more to the magistrate, who collects a large sum of money for the violation of the laws of this Christian land. The simple Chinaman cannot see that all this may exist, and still the teaching of the missionary be right. It is quite certain that the habit of gambling could be checked much easier if we had none of it among ourselves, but it is a good

The Story of China In Canada

thing to know that when a Chinaman is thoroughly taught in the principles' of Christ, and when his heart is regenerated, he at once turns away from the gaming table forever.

But the greatest vice of the Chinese is the use of opium. There was a. time when the Chinese were not addicted to this habit to any great extent, and then they were alive to the fearful effect of the drug; but when the trade in opium began to flourish in India Britain bethought herself that China would be an excellent and exhaustless market. The Chinese Government opposed the trade, but the British merchant was persistent, and the deadly work went on till at last the Chinese applied the boycott to the extent that the English merchants could not secure the necessary help to carry on their business.

At the end of six weeks the Canton merchants were compelled to capitulate, and surrender their opium, amounting to twenty thousand two hundred and ninety- one packages, valued at eleven million dollars. The Chinese received it at the river and there dumped it into the water, which resulted in the destruction of large quantities of fish, as it floated out to sea and poisoned the waters. But the people were not to be poisoned, at least by that death dealing cargo.

After this the Emperor was urged to grant licenses for the sale of it, but be it remembered to his honor he most emphatically refused the request, saying, "I can never consent to derive an income from the vices of my subjects."

When one remembers such a statement one feels that the whole liquor licensing system of our own country is rebuked, and branded as a system worse than heathen. Out of this refusal and the attitude of the Government of China on this question arose the war of 1842.

The destruction of the property of the Canton merchants was a serious matter, which led to an international conflict, the outcome of which was that the Chinese, at the point of the bayonet, were compelled to pay England an indemnity of six million dollars for the goods destroyed, and also to open five of her ports for foreign trade, and to cede the island of Hong Kong to the British forever. The degenerate son of the former Emperor yielded to the pressure of the merchant of opium, and the dark flood of death rolled over the yellow millions of China. Large tracts of land are now devoted to poppy farming with the result that the ground is being impoverished, while the people are sinking into a condition of bestiality which it is impossible to describe.

MR. AND MRS. JOHN LEE,
Members of the Methodist Church and workers among their fellow countrymen in Toronto.

No matter how loyal one may be to Britain, her flag and constitution, one cannot condone the part she played in foisting upon China a traffic which has been the cause of the untimely death of millions, to say nothing of the poverty and starvation which have been the lot of multitudes of women and

The Story of China In Canada

little children. This vice the Chinese are practising among us in Canada. In the larger towns of this country there are Chinese opium shops, where the raw and prepared article can be purchased, and the business is a most lucrative one. Every Chinatown has its opium precinct, where the dens are filled with the victims of the unspeakable habit.

Below the streets and in gloomy cellars these places are to be found, for it seems that the opium smoker instinctively craves solitude, where he can fall into his dreams of paradise, from which he will awake to find that it is turned into an awful gehenna. The effects of the drug are not the same as are generally seen in the case of one intoxicated with alcohol, which excites to madness or hilarity, but the smoker falls into a dreamy, semi-conscious condition, which prevents the perpetration of the crimes which so often attend the drunken debauch. The crime of the opium fiend falls principally on himself in the destruction of all those powers which go to make him a man above the beast; and, while it is not true that all reach such a stage of degradation, this is the tendency, and few once entangled ever shake themselves free.

The prepared drug is in the form of a thick syrup, and it is carried generally in a bottle. In the homes of the wealthy, couches are most luxuriantly furnished, where the smoker reclines with his little table and outfit near his face. The outfit consists of the horn or china bottle containing the drug. The pipe is in the form of the old-fashioned stone ink bottle, with the mouth inserted in a hollow bamboo which forms the stem. Through the centre of the bottom of the pipe is a small hole, and about this is piled the opium after it has been half roasted at a little lamp, or taper, which is kept near. The gluey substance when roasted is piled about the small hole in the bottom of the pipe, and when sufficient is roasted it is held to the flame of the lamp and the fumes of the burning drug drawn through the stem into the lungs and nostrils. This process is continued until the smoker falls asleep to dream of heaven, but to awake in hell. The Chinese temperament is such that opium seems to be, when once tasted, almost irresistible, and besotted by it, in the majority of cases death is the only end.

The appearance of an opium fiend is one which cannot well be forgotten. There comes over the countenance a strange uncanny glance, as if the victim was haunted by the demon visitants seen after the last debauch. The eyeballs seem to grow smaller and to fall back and down in the red-rimmed socket. The brow becomes wrinkled, and the lips parched and tight drawn over the teeth. The yellow skin of the Chinese opium fiend becomes of a leathery tinge, and as the disease becomes more advanced the very flesh disappears, leaving little but the living skin-covered skeleton. But between this stage and the one which marks the occasional indulgence, the experience alternates between heat and cold, paradise and perdition.

It is fervently to be hoped that something of a more radical nature will be done for the rescue of these people from this most destructive business. A law might be passed making it a crime for anyone to smoke opium; for while the prohibition of the liquor traffic presents legislative difficulties that are not easy to surmount, the prohibition of the use of opium, as it is used by the Chinese and a few others, would' at present be an easy matter.

There are those who would name a third vice which the Chinese have brought to us, viz., the procuring, by purchase, of young women from their own country for immoral purposes; but this is an evil of small dimensions at the present time, and as far as we are aware there is not sufficient evidence to show that the Chinese are, as a nation, more given to immoral practices than other heathen peoples. That this vice exists there can be no doubt, but that these people are in this matter worse than those who come to our shores from other heathen lands we do not believe; therefore, it would be unjust to place this vice side by side with that of gambling and the opium habit, which are evils rampant among Chinese.

With the strong protest which has been offered against any people who will not assimilate with us in this land we are quite in accord. The Chinese come to our shores to return to their own land at the earliest opportunity, and in such a land as ours, seeking to increase its permanent population, this is looked upon as an evil. But it is well to remember that it is the spirit of patriotism instinctive in the breast of the Mongolian which keeps his eyes on his own land.

There is something in such a spirit which finds an echo in our own souls. We, too, love our land better than all the world beside, and we are ever ready to remove hats to the poet who sung:

> "Breathes there a man with soul so dead
> Who never to himself has said
> This is my own, my native land?"

Why then consider it an evil characteristic in the Chinese that, like Joseph of old, they give orders that if buried outside of their fatherland their bones are to be returned, to rest where the generations to be may offer due reverence to their memories? Much as we may desire those who come to remain and become a part of this new and rising nation, we must prize the spirit which holds to this, or to any other land, the heart which learned first to beat there. This instinct of patriotism has been one of the most valuable assets in the nation to which we belong, and it is the instinct which has had much to do in holding the Chinese nation together through the ages which have seen the rise and fall of scores of other peoples.

But it is wise for us to glance at some of the good qualities of these "strangers within our gates." And first among these good qualities is the willingness to work for a living. This is one of the first essentials in the making of a good citizen. The lands where idleness has been the rule—where the conditions were such that nature, with little aid, made ample provision for the needs of mankind—are the countries where we find the nations which have made the poorest showing in the march of the world's civilization. On the other hand, the people who have had to work, and who have been willing to toil, have been those who have carved their way upward, or at least have been the most able to hold their own against the many disintegrating forces which have wiped from the maps of the world whole generations, and even nations.

This is another element in the nature of the Chinaman which sets him in a position to command the respect of those who look deeper into the world's history than to the mere local and temporary. Through several years, in the city of Victoria,

B.C., we were never asked for alms by the Chinese but once, and the other Chinese, who knew of this yellow beggar, declared that he was crazy or he would work for his living. That there are thousands of beggars in China we are well aware, but this was the only case in that city, with some five thousand Chinese. It is safe to say that there is a smaller percentage of idle ones among the Chinese who have come to our Dominion than can be found among any other class of foreigners. The Chinaman is willing to turn his hand to anything, so long as he can make a living and hasten the time of his departure to his own land.

As we have pointed out elsewhere, this undeveloped land may well make use of these unskilled laborers in the felling of our forests, the uncovering of our mineral deposits, and in many other lines of labor where human muscle will for all ages be at a premium.

Another virtue is seen in the native docility of the Chinese character. These people are, as a class, not vicious and turbulent. The police records will show that, with the one exception of gambling, they stand as well in the black column of the nation's crime as any people we have. One reason for this is the fact that they are not given to the use of intoxicating drink, that greatest criminal producer. Surely, while we must deplore the vices mentioned, it is a redeeming feature that we have not to rescue these people from the curse of the drink habit. During three years in the West we never saw a single Chinese under the influence of drink. No doubt such a thing does occur, and one cannot but wonder that, as matters are in this land, more of these men do not indulge.

We cannot but speak of the desire of these people for education. This is most reassuring to those who desire to do the best for their fellow men. It need not be denied that, for the most part, their desire for an education is that they may speak our language, and in that way be in a position to carry on their business, but that being the case they will be all the better citizens if they become, even in a very narrow sense, familiar with our literature. This will open to them doors which will lead them into the larger life of the Anglo-Saxon nations. Could all these people read our literature, they would then get in touch with our ideals, and learn the reasons for our opposition to their presence in this land. They would be in a better position to see themselves as others see them, and with this would come, of necessity, the desire to be our equals in the upbuilding of this land.

Rev J.C. Speer

THE CHURCH AND THE CHINESE

The First Chinese Baptized in Toronto

THE work of the Christian Church among the Chinese in Canada began in such a way as to show that the Lord who redeemed us all was the Saviour of the Chinese as well as of ourselves. In the Missionary Report for the year 1885-6 we have a brief sketch of this work, written by Rev. Dr. A. Sutherland, then, as now, General Secretary of Missions. Among other things Dr. Sutherland wrote as follows: "It has been a standing reproach of the churches that in all the years since Chinese emigrants first came to our shores nothing has been done to give them the Gospel. This reproach is now wiped away. The providence of God has opened a way to this hitherto neglected people, and the voice of the Master is heard, saying, 'They need not depart: give ye them to eat' The leadings of providence in this matter are worth recounting. More than a year ago, Mr. Dillon, of Montreal, was on the Pacific Coast, and his heart was stirred by the spiritually destitute, condition of the Chinese in Victoria. On his return he wrote to the Hon. Senator Ferrier, a member of the General Missionary Board, asking- if something could not be done, and offering, if a mission were begun, to give a donation of $100 toward its support. The letter was laid by Mr. Ferrier before the General Board, and after clue consideration it was resolved to open a school and mission among the Chinese of Victoria as soon as a suitable agent could be found. At that time a young man named Gardiner, the son of a Presbyterian missionary who had spent twenty-three years in China, was living in San Francisco. The preceding part of his life had been spent in the Flowery Kingdom, and he spoke Cantonese like a native. Early last spring Mr. Gardiner received a letter from a Chinese firm in Victoria, asking him to come up and interpret for them in a suit which was shortly to be tried. He responded to the invitation, and while in Victoria, saw how spiritually destitute was the condition of the Chinese in that city. He strove to enlist the co-operation of the local churches in behalf of a union mission, but without success. He then turned to the Methodists, from whom he received some encouragement. Enquiries were set on foot in regard to a suitable building for a school, the number who would be likely to attend, and the amount of support that would be given."

The school was organized, as the report goes on to say, and for the sum of $80 a place was rented from a Chinaman, and under Mr. Gardiner, with several ladies who offered their services, the good work became most popular. From that time to the present the work has been pressed forward not only by the assistance which has been freely given by the Board of Missions, but through all the years there has been a faithful and efficient band of elect women who have given themselves at great sacrifice to the work of bringing these Chinamen to the light and experience of salvation.

How often one is asked the question, "What good has it done?" In too many cases the tone of the interrogation makes it clear that the questioner has a conviction that the work has been in vain. But this is not the case, as all who have been for any length of time in contact with it will testify. It should be remembered that the conditions are of the very worst. The unsettled life led by the Chinese is a serious drawback to the work of the missionary. Then the moral forces are of necessity opposed to the best work among these people, who are not only foreigners, but in the most painful sense homeless. It is asserted by those who know best that the heathen have no word which exactly corresponds with our word "Home," and if this is true when they are in their native land, how much more true is it in this land, where the majority of these men herd together for years, lacking the blessed restraints of wives and children.

But the greatest obstacle in the way of the salvation of the foreigner arises from the inconsistency of many nominal Christians with whom the Chinaman meets every day in the business of life. The average heathen takes all who speak the Anglo-Saxon tongue as Christians, and when he compares the teaching of the missionary with, the actions of these so-called followers of Christ, he is so perplexed that it is almost impossible to clear from his mind the thought that a man is not a Christian simply because he believes that the Bible is true. This stands as the supreme difficulty of mission work, not only in foreign lands, but right in our own most Christian country.

ONE OF OUR CHINESE CLASSES AND ITS TEACHERS.

But notwithstanding these obstacles, the work among the Chinese went forward from stage to stage till a commodious brick church took the place of the rented rooms, and the Mission Board appointed a duly ordained minister to take charge of the work, to be assisted by teachers, both paid and volunteer. Throughout all these years the Methodists of all the Coast cities have given most valuable aid to the work of saving the Chinese, and the history of home mission work can afford no examples of greater devotion than may be cited of those to whom we refer.

That the work has been successful we are prepared to assert, and examples could be given which would more than fill the space at our disposal. Several years ago one, Ma Mou, gave his heart to God under the blessed influence of the Word and the Spirit. His life was one of singular purity from the day of his conversion, and the influence which he exerted on those with whom he lived and labored was of the most inspiring character. He was clear on the cardinal teachings of the New Testament, and his daily life tallied well with what he professed. It seemed sad that almost in the prime of his manhood he was marked for death, but his new life was a power which made him the conqueror through Christ. Not only was he fearless of death but the instinct of the intelligent Christian was strong, and it was found that this will provided that a considerable amount of property was bequeathed to our Missionary Society, and is still a source of income to our work on the Pacific Coast.

One of the young men who gave his heart to God and his life to the cause of missions came to the writer and left with him his will, when he was to be absent on an extended journey. In the document, written in broken English, it was provided that in case of his death the whole of his possessions should go to our mission work, under the direction of the General Board. We cite these instances to show that while the Chinese are looked upon by some as mercenary in disposition, when the power of the Lord Jesus fills their hearts they are made large and disposed to devise liberal things for the cause which has been instrumental in bringing them from darkness to light.

We think of another young man who suffered much for the Gospel's sake. He was the proprietor of one of the largest Chinese laundry plants in the place, and when converted he was compelled to make several changes. Images of heathen gods were taken down, and the workmen were offended that they could not have these gods before them while they worked; but Chan Sui felt that, since he was a Christian, his business should have no trace of false gods. Then there were certain practices among the men which he felt it his duty to abolish. This was another cause of trouble, and threats were made that he would fail to get the necessary help if he did not allow these doings; but this "Washee-washee-man" was firm to the last, and the evils were abolished. Then he found that it was inconsistent with the "new life" to work on the Lord's Day, although not a few Christian people demanded that their laundry be brought home and taken away on Sunday. This meant the diminishing of his business to a point where it would be impossible to make large profits, but here again lie took the stand of the true servant of Jesus Christ, and his place of business was silent for one day in seven.

But before him was a greater trial than all. Chan Sui was one of the few Chinamen who brought with him his wife, but nothing could persuade her to turn from her heathen religion. Long and faithfully did the converted husband pray and try to induce her to turn to the religion in which he had found so much joy and hope, but all to no purpose. Her mind was dark and her heart was hard, and at last so bitter did she become that she forsook her home and fell into evil habits. At length she returned to China, and from information received it was evident that she had sunk to the lowest depths. To the forsaken husband this was a severe trial, "for there was now, if never before, the true love of a faithful husband for a wife, and it seemed that the sun of his life had set but shortly after it had arisen. But in the midst of this sore distress he found that the new power which had come into his life was sufficient to sustain him to, the uttermost, and his faith never faltered. To this day he is a true and humble follower of the Lord by whose grace he was rescued from the darkness of heathenism and brought into the liberty and light of the Gospel.

Among such examples one cannot overlook one of the most conspicuous, in the case of Tong Chue Tom. He was one of the Chinese who came in the early days to find gold in the mountains of our far West, but the task was beyond his strength, or so it has been said, and he turned back from the Cariboo Mountains to find work as a navvy on the Canadian Pacific Railway, which, at the time of his coming, was being completed to the coast. But may we not say, in the light of subsequent events, that the providence of God turned him back that he might be set in the way by which he would become a man of God for the special mission to which his life has been given.

MR. AND MRS. TONG CHUE THOM,
Methodist Missionaries, New Westminster, B.C.

From the position of a common navvy he went to find employment as a house servant in the home of one of the elect women of the Methodist Church in the City of New Westminster, through whose faithfulness and teaching he was ultimately led to the light and experience of salvation. Many were the obstacles to be overcome, and severe were the trials to be endured by the lonely Chinese boy, who experienced the bitterness of persecution from those who had been all their lives under the influences of Christian civilization. But he was faithful to the end of the persecutions, for they did come to an end, and none in the city where he found salvation, and where he has been in charge of the Chinese mission work for several years, but accord to him the respect due to a Christian of the most sterling quality.

It is only fair to say that it was this young man who is mentioned above as making his will for the benefit of the Missionary Society, should anything befall him on a somewhat extended journey. To our work he is worth more than all his money. It would do many people good to read their own epitaph while yet alive.

Among the agencies of our Church one cannot forget the work done by the Woman's Missionary Society on the Coast. Perhaps in nothing was it so conspicuous as in the rescue of girls and women who were wrongly, and. for evil purposes, brought to our country. These unfortunate creatures were in many cases no better than slaves, and the lives which they were compelled to live were in many cases much worse. But our W. M. S. opened a home of refuge for such as could be induced to enter, and although at no time was there a large number of such in the home, and perhaps in the aggregate the numbers rescued throughout the years are not as large ·as some would expect, still, those who have been in touch with the work will be prepared to declare that the number rescued would not fully indicate the total benefit- done through the institution.

One of the indirect benefits, of incalculable value to the country, was seen in the deterring effect the "Home" had upon those who were engaged in importing these characters to our shores. When a slave girl was taken from her possessor by the strong arm of the law, at the instance of the Rescue Home, and when the case was pursued from court to court till the victim was set free forever- from her owner, it was effective in deterring others from entering a business which spelled to them financial disaster. Not a few of these girls were innocent and were the victims of the kidnapper, and when they were not only rescued from the hands of a tyrant, but through the care and teaching of the Home were led to Christ, the work was not to be overlooked nor belittled. Some of these girls were afterward married to Chinese, and began home-keeping as Christians and citizens of this Dominion.

The streets were deep with mud, but the sun was shining, as we passed through the streets of Chinatown. Not far from the Joss House we encountered a knot of Chinese gathered on the sidewalk, while ankle-deep in the mud was one of their own countrymen. While we halted to take in the situation, and learn just what they were at on this Sunday afternoon, the man in the muddy street began to sing in a broken accent:

> " Jesus loves me, this I know,
> For the Bible tells me so."

Then he interpreted the verse to the listening company and sang it in the Cantonese tongue. While he was singing, another stepped out by his side and took up the song, and together they made the streets ring with the sweet refrain:

> "Yes, Jesus loves me,
> Yes, Jesus loves me,
> Yes, Jesus loves me,
> The Bible tells me so."

At the close of the simple hymn there was a short prayer offered, and then the first man began to tell to the people the story of the love of God who sent His Son to this world to seek and to save the lost.

While he was speaking the rumble of the conjurer's drum could be heard in the Joss House hard by, and mingled with the song of salvation we could distinctly hear the liquid notes of the tongueless bells from the place of idol worship. The little street service went on, and while another hymn was being sung a third Chinaman joined the two, and there the three converts stood before their countrymen telling to them the wonderful story of life. Their fire and power in address would have satisfied an old time Methodist, while there was in it all that deep tone which told that they knew by experience the story whereof they affirmed.

As the service closed, and these three held a brief consultation as to the open air work in which they had united, we were deeply touched with the fact that here was found true unity among men of different Christian denominations. The man to open the service was the teacher in the mission of the Presbyterian Church, the second was a lay worker in the Methodist mission, and the third held the same position in the Anglican work of the city; all three missions working side by side in Chinatown, and here all three engaged in this open air evangelistic work. This was one of the most blessed sights it was ever the privilege of the writer to witness, and it seemed to be a prophecy of what is to be. As the company dispersed on that spring day it seemed that the Christianity which had been sung and preached would give tongue yet to the tongueless bells of the far East, and they would ring out to all the world the truth proclaimed in that street service:

"Jesus loves me, this I know."

The work which began in the City of Victoria, B.C., soon spread to other cities of the Coast, and it has in these later years reached in some form, most of the towns and villages of the interior where the Chinamen are to be found in any considerable numbers. Still later, and much too late we think, the towns in the East have undertaken the work of teaching these humble heathen the way of life. But it is the thought of those who have had some experience that but little can be done till the various Mission Boards take the matter into their plans of mission work for the foreigners who have come to our shores. Thousands of these people are to be found in Ontario, and they are as sheep without a shepherd. They may well say, when they realize what it all means, "No man cared for my soul." In the larger cities a few faithful souls, at their own charges, have fostered this work, and under great difficulties have tried to keep in touch with these Mongolians, but at best such work must be of a haphazard character.

China is now awake, and she will never again relapse into the slumber of the past. When she fully realizes her power, like a giant she will be a most formidable foe if she should ever become a military power in the Orient. While we write tens of thousands of Chinese are being trained in the art and business of war. The inexhaustible resources of the Celestial Empire would supply her with material for war, so that she would be practically unconquerable. Her soldiery could live on one-third what the European or American soldier would need while on the field. While the Chinese have not, for centuries, been known as warriors, it is a fact that they fear death no more than do their brothers of Japan, and while at present they seem to lack initiative and the ability of administration, these elements can be secured, and may be producible quantities to a degree that is not now believed.

In the problem of that great people there seems to be one essential as a first condition of future safety and greatness, and that is the Gospel of the Son of God. Toward this solution the conversion of the Chinese who are in this country will be a contribution, the magnitude of which no one can easily estimate.

METHODS OF WORK, PAST AND FUTURE

Leaving Old China

IN the past the Church in her missionary work has not overlooked the Chinese who have come to our shores, and eternity alone will tell the results of the teaching in the schools where these men congregate. The Chinese find themselves seriously handicapped with our language, and their wage earning power is reduced to a minimum because of their lack of "the business tongue." Their first and most ardent desire therefore, is to become able to speak and write in English. This is a fortunate circumstance, for the mission teacher can lay hold upon the darkest as well as the brightest minds while teaching them the Word of Eternal Life. Perhaps it is a very human impulse which moves them when they come to the mission school. They know little, and care less, about the aims of the missionary, so long as they can get acquainted with our "talkee, talkee."

But following the admonition to "be wise as serpents and harmless as doves," the mission school teacher knows well that here is an open door to minds otherwise securely closed to the truth and light of the Gospel. Accordingly the Missionary Society—under the inspiration of such men as Mr. Dillon, of Montreal, and the late Senator Sanford, of Hamilton, whose name should not be overlooked in this connection—established a work in Victoria, B.C., which has grown into several most successful schools, where hundreds of Chinese are being taught, night after night, year in and year out, the rudiments of an English education, .and at the same time the teachings of the Word of God. This work has been in a measure successful, and we think it has fully repaid all the money we have expended upon it, and the loving labor of the faithful few who have given their time and talents toward this enlightenment.

The method of work is simplicity itself, for nothing of an elaborate kind could be successful. A comfortable room which will accommodate without crowding, a few tables, a blackboard, with maps of China, and our own country, and one of the Holy Land constitute almost the entire plant. The work which has been done in these schools has been, generally speaking, the teaching of the English alphabet, followed by the Chinese-English primer. After the pupil can read the simplest words, hymns and simple Scripture lessons are given, and in this way the willing student at last becomes acquainted not only with our tongue, written and spoken, but with the Gospel in our hymns and in the Bible itself.

It has been found necessary, in most cases, to give one teacher to each pupil, and to this method the average Chinaman takes with much better grace than to the class work. The time to teach a man or boy to read fairly well varies with the conditions of the individual, but in any case it is one of the most tedious and trying of tasks in mission work. But one thing is ever evident, the Chinese are eager to learn, and they have little or no prejudice against the rule that makes the Bible the basis of their work. After a half hour spent in the closest study the services of the session begin, and all are encouraged to remain and to take some part.

At first it is all mystery to the late arrival, but he has the encouragement of those who have been longer here, and who understand something of what it all means; and of late years, in all our missions, there are those who are as zealous for the salvation of their countrymen as the best of us could be. Soon they learn to sing the hymns which are before them on the hangers, on which they are printed in both languages. I think it is the exception when any teacher has had to reprove any of these heathen men for misconduct, or even inattention at times of devotion.

The Ten Commandments and the Sermon on the Mount are to be so mastered that they can be recited, and one of the most unique entertainments is when the recitations are totally from the Bible. Boy after boy will take his place and recite whole chapters of the Word of God. We think only once did we hear a Chinaman give anything at an entertainment but Bible recitations, and that time he had mastered a patriotic poem on Canada. One of the pleasing features of this work is the willingness of these men to contribute of their means for the support of the mission. In one charge they have for years subscribed hundreds of dollars to the cause of missions.

Perhaps one of the mightiest factors in this work is the personal contact of the devout Christian teacher with the dark-minded heathen. For the most part the teachers are those whose hearts have been filled with the Holy Spirit, and they see that in the presence of these godless people the foreign mission field has been brought to our very doors. Many who could not go to the foreign mission field see that the work has been brought within reach, and that "the fields are white unto harvest." In the foreign cities of China there is little or no need, and therefore no desire, to learn the English language, but here it becomes the golden key to unlock the fast closed doors of the heathen mind.

It is doubtful, indeed, whether there be, in the wide range of foreign mission work, any opening so opulent of advantages as among these benighted thousands of willing seekers after light. Many of them return to their native land, and when visiting their relatives and former neighbors they are sure to convey to them the knowledge they have gained of the Word of God, and of the blessings of salvation. Not a few of them follow the example of the teachers who led them to the truth, and begin on their, native soil the work of missions. This was the case on the day of Pentecost, when the converts went everywhere telling the story of their salvation, and the same is true in the case of the converts of the present day.

It is said that the only thing the average Chinaman takes back to China, excepting the money he has saved, is his knowledge of English, and that the most devout Christians while here, under the eye of the missionary, abandon it all when they come in contact with their own countryman, who despise all things foreign. In answer to this we may say that the Chinese are like other mortals, not all of the same stamina and courage, but there are some facts which go to show that the Christian Chinaman can fearlessly stand for the faith which he has espoused. In the fierce Boxer massacres we have evidences which may well forever shut the mouths who affect to despise the moral courage of the Chinese. In these fearful months of carnage it is shown that no less than 28,000 of the Christian Chinese gave up their lives for their faith, "not accepting deliverance." The offering of a smoking punk-stick to the idol would have been quite sufficient to have bought their release, but, no! they rejoiced that they were counted worthy to suffer for the cause of Jesus Christ.

The long roll of Christian martyrs has in its lists none more worthy than these yellow Mongolian followers of our Lord Jesus Christ.

He is not a critic to be feared who rises to ask the question, "Are we doing, in means and methods, the best we can do in this work?" I think we are not, and those most responsible for the work will agree that we should be doing more and better for these people. It must be remembered that the Missionary Society of our Church has confined its benefactions to the four or five stations on the Pacific Coast. In the rest of the Dominion, from that Western province to Newfoundland, there are to be found in every important town and city from fifty to five hundred Chinese.

These people huddle together in a common centre through the winter months, from which they move to the adjoining villages, where they can find work in the summer time, when the laundry business flourishes. It is true that a few schools have been started here and there, and volunteer teachers have struggled with the problem, but for the most part the work has been spasmodic, and the results correspondingly meagre. It seems strange that we, who are so anxious to make one convert in the Empire of China, have left uncultivated such fertile soil in the Dominion of Canada. The fault is not that the Missionary Society would be reluctant to move in a matter so important, but that the question has never been pressed upon the attention of the General Board of Missions, where the question of new enterprises must be initiated.

Perhaps the reason that this matter has never, as far as we have heard, been urged upon our missionary authorities, is due to the thought that the work outside the few centres in the West is not of sufficient importance to demand special attention, But we venture to assert that even on the basis of the financial, no work in which we can engage will yield so large returns in Christian character for the money necessary in the case.

The first trouble with all the Chinese work in this country is that it lacks the inspiration of a central personality who shall keep in touch with the teachers and Chinese converts. This person and office is as essential to the success of the work as they are to the other departments. The men who are sent to China will not be able to accomplish more for the cause of God among their teeming millions than could the man under whose guidance this work could be carried forward in our own land.

We should be able to provide a literature for these converts, so that they would get into the heart of our national life, and, while at first this would have to be of a very simple character, it would serve to keep pernicious literature at bay or at least neutralize its effects. We may be certain that as soon as we teach these men to read our language they will begin to widen the range of their investigations.

The money necessary for this extra work would be but little when compared with the expenditure necessary to accomplish as much, or less, in a foreign land. There would be no cost for new buildings. Our churches are already provided for all kinds of Christian effort. The work of teaching will always be of a volunteer character, but as things are there is no head to the movement, and there never will be till that head is created by the only appointing power in our Church.

Another department, which is not absolutely new, should be the appointment of a school superintendent wherever there are sufficient Chinese to form a class from which a Chinese Sunday School might be developed. This, in an unofficial way, is now done in a few places, but there has been no encouragement to the work and those who have undertaken it have received no official recognition. The inclusion of this work with the ordinary Sunday School will be to court failure, as the methods necessary in each are vastly different. The Chinese have a most profound reverence for those who bear official authority, and it means much to those who labor among them that they are the appointed representatives of the church.

MR. AND MRS. CHAN YU TAN AND FAMILY,
Our Chinese Missionaries in Vancouver, B.C.

These schools have always paid their way, and in some of them they have not failed to contribute to other departments of the Church enterprises. This work might well and successfully be coupled with the mission work we are now doing among the Japanese who are in the country, and while the schools and services would necessarily be separate, the one superintendent would be sufficient for the whole field.

The Forward Movement, which has inspired our young people to such success along the line of foreign mission work, might be turned to this also with great profit to themselves and to these redeemed heathen who live among us. There is likely to be a rapid influx of the best farmer class from Japan, where the arable area is very small. These will be no menace to the people of our Dominion; they will be a thrifty and frugal people, whose only reason for coming to us will be because of the excessive crowding in the rural districts of their own country. Already there are Japanese gentlemen who have under consideration the problem of the settlement of thousands of these people on the lands of the West - and in the valleys of British Columbia. That such people should be welcomed by us will not now be questioned, and as the Church exists for the purpose of preaching the Gospel to every creature, it behooves us to prepare for the work we have here and for its enlargement when occasion commands us to the task.

As these two peoples have been the special object of our foreign mission policy in their native countries, we should lay our hand to a fuller extent upon those who have come within our doors and are glad to hearken to the Word of Life.

"In the lands of gloom beyond us,
Where life's burden breaks the heart,
Gasping in the tyrant's fingers,
Pierced by Superstition's dart,
Wait the millions for the message
Christ has sent us to impart.

" Who may halt when Christ calls, 'Forward!'
When to falter means to fail?
Who, with ears so dull of hearing,
Cannot catch the dying wail
Coming over sea and mountain?
Shall its pathos not prevail ?"

www.ingramcontent.com/pod-product-compliance
Lightning Source LLC
Chambersburg PA
CBHW070036040426
42333CB00040B/1689